Students and External Readers	Staff & Research Students
DATE DUE FOR RETURN	**DATE OF ISSUE**

28 JUN 1973

28. 06. 90

18. MAR 93

Any book which you borrow remains your responsibility until the loan slip is cancelled

CARLYLE AND HITLER

LONDON
Cambridge University Press
FETTER LANE

NEW YORK · TORONTO
BOMBAY · CALCUTTA · MADRAS
Macmillan

TOKYO
Maruzen Company Ltd

CARLYLE & HITLER

THE ADAMSON LECTURE IN
THE UNIVERSITY OF MANCHESTER
DECEMBER 1930

with
some additions and modifications

by

H. J. C. GRIERSON
LL.D., Litt.D., F.B.A.
*Professor of Rhetoric and English Literature
in the University of Edinburgh*

CAMBRIDGE
AT THE UNIVERSITY PRESS
1933

PRINTED IN GREAT BRITAIN

NOTE

This lecture was delivered three years ago as *Carlyle and the Hero*, and has been little modified or added to since, despite many good intentions. But I have been tempted to give it a new, shall I say metonymous, title, so entirely do the recent happenings in Germany illustrate the conditions which lead up to, or at least make possible, the emergence of the Hero as Carlyle chiefly thought of him, and the feelings, religious and political (including economic), which raise the wave that washes him into power. It will be seen that I pass no judgment upon that movement, but I do not think it fair to make the University of Manchester responsible for my choice of title. It is not my own opinions I have tried to develop but those of Carlyle as seen in the perspective afforded by the course of events since the War.

H. J. C. G.

Who ere thou beest that read'st this sullen Writ
    Which just as much courts thee, as thou dost it,
Let me arrest thy thoughts; wonder with mee,
    Why ploughing, building, ruling and the rest,
Or most of those arts whence our lives are blest,
    By cursed Cain's race invented be,
And blest Seth vext us with Astronomie [i.e. Astrology].
    There's nothing simply good, nor ill alone,
Of every quality Comparison
    The only measure is, and judge Opinion.

JOHN DONNE
The Progresse of the Soule

CARLYLE AND HITLER

I was much struck, writes Carlyle to Emerson in 1853, some two years after the publication of *Latter Day Pamphlets* had shocked many of his most sincere admirers: "I was much struck with Plato and his ideas about Democracy, mere *Latter Day Pamphlets* saxa et faces (read *faeces*, if you like) refined into empyrean radiance and lightning of the Gods!—I for my part perceive the use of all this too, the inevitability of all this; but perceive it at the present height it has attained to be disastrous withal, to be horrible and even damnable. That Judas Iscariot should come and slap Jesus Christ on the shoulder in a familiar manner; that all heavenly nobleness should be flung out into the muddy streets there to jostle elbows with all the thickest-skinned denizens of Chaos, and get itself at every turn trampled into the gutters and annihilated: alas, the reverse of all this was, and is, and ever will be the strenuous effort and solemn heart purpose of every good citizen in every country of the world, and will reappear conspicuously as such (in New England and in Old first of all) when once this malodorous melancholy Uncle-Tommey is got all put by!

which will take some time yet I think". So, in words as forcible as if they had been spoken by the author of *Also Sprach Zarathustra*, does Carlyle express his sincere conviction regarding the advent of Democracy as he sees it pouring in through the sluices successively opened by Whig, Radical, Tory and Liberal alike. But if Carlyle's contempt is as sincere and as vehemently expressed as that of Nietzsche he arrived at that conviction from a different angle of approach. It is with no naturally aristocratic contempt for the lower orders, or Junker's hardness of temper, that he speaks; quite otherwise. Carlyle did not share, he had not much respect for, Shakespeare's and Scott's ambition to win for themselves a place among those privileged beings who bear coats of arms, whom birth and fortune allow to cultivate the graces and splendours of life, a life that whatever its faults has a certain aesthetic appeal, the appeal of distinction if it be only of manner and tradition. Of the Scottish nobility he writes, after reading *Tales of a Grandfather*, "Lastly, it is noteworthy that the nobles of this country have maintained a quite despicable behaviour from the time of Wallace downwards. A selfish, famishing, unprincipled set of hyaenas, though toothless now, still mischievous and greedy beyond limit". Later indeed he said more than once in conversation that it was among the

10

English nobility he had met on the whole the best specimens of humanity this country had to show.

But it was with no aristocratic prejudice that Carlyle became the critic and foe of democracy; quite the opposite. The humour or temper of the young peasant who tramped to Edinburgh University and, turning away from the Presbyterian Ministry, spent bitter years in teaching, translating, hack-work of every kind, and spiritual wrestling, was more akin, he confesses, to that of a Sansculotist. You remember his description of Professor Teufelsdroeckh: "lifting his large tumbler of Gug-guk, and for a moment lowering his tobacco-pipe, he stood up in full coffee-house...and there with low soul-stirring tone and the look truly of an angel, though whether of a white or of a black one might be dubious, proposed this toast: *die Sache der Armen in Gottes und Teufels Namen*—the cause of the poor in Heaven's name and the —'s".

Die Sache der Armen, the cause of the poor, was Carlyle's abiding preoccupation, the inspiring motive of almost everything he wrote, but it did *not* make him a democrat or a philanthropist of the kind he saw around him, interested in the negroes of Borrioboolah Gha, or Jamaica, or the criminals in model prisons at home. Negroes were happiest, he thought, when made to work;

11

and model prisons and poor-houses were the sores, the scabs, which betrayed a deeper seated disease. It was not by doctoring the scabs at the expense of the struggling tax-payer that the disease was to be cured. It was his diagnosis of the disease that led him away from his friends, the whole Manchester school of *laissez-faire* and the Radicals—"Hide-bound Radicalism; to me a well-nigh insupportable thing—a breath as of the Sahara and the Infinite Sterile". It was this that brought him to a position not very remote from that of Nietzsche, if the spirit which animates it be different, if he demands the rule of the best not for *their* sake but for the sake of the poor, the victims of *laissez-faire*. But to understand Carlyle's political position and his doctrine of the Hero, of the relation of Might to Right, requires some consideration of the history of his thought.

For the best of a man's thinking is the work of his early years and this is pre-eminently true of the Prophet. When Christ entered on his three years' mission it was no longer as a learner but as a teacher: One who spake "with authority and not as the Scribes and Pharisees". Mohammed "was forty before he talked of any mission from Heaven". But thereafter he knew what his mission was. "I had a good talk", says Emerson, "with Carlyle last night. He says over and over for months, for years, the same thing." But that is the note of the Prophet. "There is one God and Mahomet is his Prophet" is the burden of the Koran. The Kingdom of Heaven in the sermons of Christ is likened unto many things.

Well, Carlyle came to Edinburgh in 1808 and was a student there till 1814. He taught for two years with Edward Irving at Kirkcaldy. From 1818 to 1822 he was tutoring, hack-writing and wrestling with dyspepsia and the devil in the beautiful but draughty city of Edinburgh. In 1822 he became tutor to the Bullers, while continuing his literary work. In 1826 he married, and two years later retreated to Craigenputtock, where he composed *Sartor Resartus*, with which one may say his *Lehrjahre* end, though there were still years of suffering and financial uncertainty to follow. By that time he had come through deep waters to the message he had to deliver, religious and social. For the two foci around which his thought moved elliptically during these years were just these—religion, what to think of the Universe in which we find ourselves, and the social problem, the "condition of the people" question, as he calls it, presented in the acute forms of these years which have been so well described recently by the Hammonds.*

* *The Village Labourer*, 1760–1882 (London, 1920) and *The Town Labourer*, 1760–1882 (London, 1925), by J. L. Hammond and Barbara Hammond.

He had parted from his early Christian moorings as completely as Schopenhauer or Nietzsche. Through regard for his old mother, he continued to use in a sense of his own the language to which she and he were accustomed, with an effect that has sometimes bewildered his readers, sometimes perhaps himself. But of that later. No reader of his life and conversation can doubt that he thought of Christianity as something that had had its day. "Jesuitism", the title of one of his *Latter Day Pamphlets*, means in the broad sense he uses it, just what he thought Coleridge and Maurice and others were busy doing, trying to discover esoteric reasons for believing what had ceased to be believable. "For the old eternal Powers do live forever; nor do their laws know any change, however we in our poor wigs and Church-tippets may attempt to read their laws. To *steal* into Heaven by the modern method of sticking ostrich-like your head into fallacies on Earth...is forever forbidden. High treason is the name of that attempt; and it continues to be punished as such." "Strange enough:" he says of Coleridge, "here once more was a kind of Heaven-scaling Ixion; and to him as to the old one the just Gods were very stern! The ever-revolving, never-advancing wheel (of a kind) was his through life; and from his Cloud-Juno did not he too procreate strange Centaurs,

14

spectral Puseyisms, monstrous illusory Hybrids, and ecclesiastical Chimeras—which now haunt the earth in a very lamentable manner!" The effect of this definite severance of old ties is the theme of the three most famous chapters of *Sartor Resartus*, and one must ask what was the faith to which in this crisis Carlyle attained. In the chapter called "The Everlasting No" he gets down to his own consciousness of good and evil, his own rejection of evil: "Thus had the Everlasting No (*das ewige Nein*) pealed authoritatively through all the recesses of my being, of my Me: and then it was that my whole Me stood up in native God-created majesty and with emphasis recorded its Protest.... The Everlasting No had said: 'Behold thou art fatherless, outcast, and the universe is mine (the Devil's)': to which my whole Me now made answer: '*I* am not thine, but Free, and forever hate thee!'" The experience is not unlike that which Professor Elton describes as the feeling with which we contemplate the close of a great moral tragedy like *King Lear*. Here is evil apparently triumphant, no solution of the mystery of things divinable, but yet we feel that we would rather be with Lear and Cordelia than with wickedness even triumphant. Whatever the moral character of the universe, the human soul remains the impregnable citadel of its own values. The next step is more difficult to follow. It is a step which Nietzsche and Schopenhauer felt unable to take, for it is a judgment about the moral character, the fundamental justice of the universe however mysterious its operations. There is a *saltus*, in faith. It is a little difficult to follow the exact implication of the "Everlasting Yea" chapter, but one may divine its trend towards an idealistic conception of God and the World for which Carlyle found support in the philosophy of the Germans, though he has none of Coleridge's interest in the *systems* of Kant or Schelling or Hegel. "Often also could I see the black Tempest marching in anger through the Distance: round some Schreckhorn, as yet grim-blue would the eddying vapour gather and there tumultuous eddy and flow down like a mad witch's hair; till, after a space, it vanished, and in the clear sunbeam your Schreckhorn stood smiling grim-white, for the vapour had held snow. How thou fermentest and elaboratest, in thy great fermenting vat and laboratory of an Atmosphere, of a World, O Nature!—Or what is Nature? Ha! why do I not name thee God? Art not thou the 'Living Garment of God?' O Heavens, is it in very deed, He, then, that ever speaks through thee; that lives and loves in thee, that lives and loves in me?"

And so from his own soul Carlyle makes the

saltus to God. The working of the Infinite in the Finite—is not that the explanation of the interminable controversy of the origin of evil? "Man's Unhappiness comes of his Greatness: it is because there is an Infinite in him which with all his cunning he cannot quite bury under the Finite. Will the whole Finance Ministers and Upholsterers and Confectioners of modern Europe undertake in joint stock company to make one shoeblack HAPPY? They cannot accomplish it above an hour or two; for the shoeblack also has a Soul quite other than his stomach...", and so *Es leuchtet mir ein*, I see a glimpse of it, "there is in man a Higher than Love of Happiness; he can do without Happiness and instead thereof find Blessedness....On the roaring billows of Time thou art not engulfed, but borne aloft into the azure of Eternity. Love not Pleasure, Love God. This is the Everlasting Yea, wherein all contradictions are solved: wherein whoso walks and works it is well with him". So Carlyle recovered for himself, or believed he had, a religious outlook on life, a faith that, inscrutable as is the nature of God, there is a meaning in the word God—there is justice at the heart of things.

Of the bearing of this on the doctrine of the Hero I shall speak, but first must consider briefly how he approached the other great problem—

the social problem, the condition of the People under the rule of industrial *laissez-faire*, the Creed of Manchester. *Die Sache der Armen in Gottes und Teufels Namen.* Carlyle came of poor people, had known the problem of poverty at almost as close quarters as Burns, and his life in Edinburgh had made him familiar with the darker fate of the industrial poor of the city. In the strange chapter in *Sartor* called the "Dandiacal Body"—for *Sartor* was in part a satire on the dandiacal novel of Lytton and Disraeli—he describes in two picturesque figures the ever-widening gulf in society between the two sects of the Dandies and the Drudges, and what it seemed to him likely to lead to; and the problem of industry and the poor was the theme of his most passionately felt work, *Past and Present*, *Chartism*, and *Latter Day Pamphlets*. The last of these with its "Nigger Question," "Model Prisons," "Hudson's Statue," "Jesuitism," etc. has been a sad choke-pear to liberal philanthropists and many of Carlyle's admirers, but, with all its extravagances, it is a central work. It is in the light of what he says there that one must read his earlier works, for in this he turned on the head-lights with illuminating if also with somewhat dazzling effect. From it, as from *Past and Present*, it becomes clear what was to Carlyle the central evil in the condition of the poor. It was

18

the effects of the great Manchester Gospel of
laissez-faire, what the Americans call "rugged
individualism". In an interesting letter of 1820,
Sir Walter Scott describes what had come about.
While industry was dependent on water power,
the manufacturer set up his mill in some country
place, and around it grew an industrial village.
He knew his workers. Their health and welfare
were his interest. His relation to them was to
some extent paternal.* With the advent of steam
and the growth of great cities, all that had dis-
appeared. The employer's relation to his hands
had become only that of a weekly wage-payer,
the only tie between them what Carlyle calls a
"cash nexus". "All this dire misery...of our
Chartisms, Trades-strikes, Toryisms, Corn-laws
and the general down-break of *Laissez-faire*...
may we not regard it as a voice from the dumb
bosom of Nature saying to us: 'Behold! Supply-

* "When the machinery was driven by water the Manufacturer had to seek out some sequestered spot where he could
obtain a suitable fall of water, and there his workmen form'd
the inhabitants of a village around him, and he necessarily
bestow'd some attention, more or less, on their morals and on
their necessities, had knowledge of their persons and characters,
and exercised over them a salutary influence as over men
depending on and intimately connected with him and his
prospects. This is now quite changed. The manufacturers are
transferd to great towns where a man may assemble 500 workmen one week and dismiss the next, without having any further
connection with them than to receive a week's work for a week's
wage, nor any further solicitude about their future fate than if
they were so many shuttles." To John B. S. Merritt, 19 May,
1820.

19

and-demand is *not* the one law of Nature; Cash-payment is *not* the sole nexus of man with man—how far from it!'...Ah me, into what waste latitudes, in this Time-voyage have we wandered; like adventurous Sinbads:—where the men go about as if by galvanism, with meaningless glaring eyes and have no soul, but only a beaver-faculty and stomach! The haggard despair of Cotton-factory hands, Coal-mine operatives...in these days is painful to behold; but not so painful, hideous to the inner-sense as that brutish, God-forgetting Profit-and-Loss philosophy and Life-theory which we hear jangled on all hands...as the Ultimate Gospel and candid Plain English of Man's Life from the throats and pens and thoughts of all but all men*....*Laissez-faire* on the part of the governing Classes, we repeat again and again, will, with whatever difficulty, have to cease; paci-

---

* "It is not by the intermeddling of Mr Southey's idol, the omniscient and omnipotent State, but by the prudence and energy of the people, that England has hitherto been carried forward in civilisation; and it is to the same energy that we now look with comfort and good hope. Our rulers will best promote the improvement of the nation by strictly confining themselves to their legitimate duties, by leaving capital to find its most lucrative course, commodities their fair price, industry and intelligence their natural reward, idleness and folly their natural punishment, by maintaining peace, by defending property, by diminishing the price of law, and by observing strict economy in every department of the state. Let the Government do this: the people will assuredly do the rest." Macaulay, "Southey's Colloquies on Society", *Edinburgh Review*, Jan. 1830.

fic mutual division of the spoil and a world well let alone will no longer suffice. A Do-nothing Guidance; and it is a Do-something World."

But it is not my purpose to discuss Carlyle's social teaching in detail, though it has acquired a new interest and significance from the social and political condition of England and Europe to-day. What I wish to indicate is that Carlyle's cult of the Hero had its roots in both his religious and his social conclusions and convictions.

Jesus Christ was not God, in the sense which he had been taught to believe—but the divine spirit was revealed in him and in other great men. "But now, if all things that we look upon are emblems to us of the Highest God, I add that more so than any of them is man such an emblem. You have heard of St Chrysostom saying in reference to the Shekinah or Ark of Testimony, visible revelation of God among the Hebrews: 'the true Shekinah is Man!' Yes, it is even so: this is no vain phrase; it is veritably so. The essence of our being, the mystery in that which calls itself I . . . is a breath of Heaven; the Highest Being reveals himself in man . . . 'there is but one Temple in the Universe', says the devout Novalis, 'and that is the Body of Man . . . we touch Heaven when we lay our hand on a human body'. . . . *We* are the miracle of miracles—the great inscrutable mystery of God. . . . And now if worship even of a star had some

21

meaning in it, how much more that of a Hero!
Worship of a Hero is transcendent admiration of
a Great Man. I say great men are still admirable;
I say there is at bottom nothing else admirable....
It is at this hour and at all hours the vivifying influence in man's life. Religion, I find, stands upon
it; not Paganism only, but far higher and truer
religions—all religion hitherto known. Hero-
worship, heart-felt, prostrate admiration, sub-
mission burning, boundless, for a noblest, god-
like Form of Man—is not that the germ of
Christianity itself? The greatest of all Heroes is
One whom we do not name here. Let sacred
silence meditate that sacred matter; you will find
it the ultimate perfection of a principle extant
throughout man's whole history on earth."

That will suffice as a statement of the religious
aspect of Carlyle's Hero-worship. Nietzsche
scoffs at the religious cast given by Carlyle to the
admiration of the Hero, but Gundolf, a disciple of
Nietzsche to some extent, but more of Stephan
George, puts the case for the Hero on much the
same basis. The opponent's case is, he says,
threefold: (1) that all greatness is relative; (2)
that past greatness has no longer significance for
us; (3) that no man has any significance beside
the Ideas or God. The case for the Hero is (1) that
all claims, traditions, conceptions are in the end
beams and emanations from great men; (2) that

there is no absolutely past but only differently effective degrees of eternity . . . (3) that there are for men no superhuman, free Ideas, that only in Man are ideas incorporate, made actual, including the Idea of God.*

But of Nietzsche and Gundolf later. I wish now to consider the relation of Carlyle's social ideas to the cult of the Hero. Looking out on the chaotic world of industrial and governmental *laissez-faire*, employers and employed connected only by a cash nexus, Government convinced that its sole

---

* The transcendental, abstract German style is always a little difficult for a sober Briton to reduce to concrete terms but I take this to mean that (1) everything of excellence to which the human race has attained whether a useful machine, a good ballad, a higher moral or spiritual standard, is ultimately due to some gifted individual; (2) that nothing is really dead, man or language or idea, which is still a moving and quickening force; (3) that only when and as they become *incarnate* are concepts capable of moving us to love or worship: "Lessing has said that in the religion of reason there is neither religion nor reason, and rightly; for religion, without fear, hope, faith and love for the Supreme Being, is impossible. A concept can arouse neither fear, hope, belief nor love. . . . In order to love beauty or the Divinity, we must feel their impress within ourselves and somehow represent them to our imagination". Vossler, *Mediaeval Culture*. The progress of religious thought and experience that led to Christianity might be described as circular—from particular, individual but imperfect, at best National, gods to a purified concept of God such as along different lines Hebrew prophet and Greek philosopher had made their way to, and thence, in the Incarnation, to an embodiment of that higher concept in a person who could be loved and worshipped. The identification of Christ with the Deity has been compared to similar deifications of heroes and emperors. It was something quite different because He became the Incarnation of an infinitely higher conception of the Godhead.

clear duty was to do as little as possible beyond keeping an open field for the mutual play or warfare of competitive forces, he found one doctrine of a cure for the accumulating evils being industriously preached—Democracy. Intensify still further this mutual warfare by giving every man a vote and mechanically the warring elements will begin to take form, to crystallise, and through the mystic machinery of the hustings and the ballot-box we shall secure the Benthamist ideal of the greatest good of the greatest number. This doctrine Carlyle regarded with contempt: "The notion that a man's liberty consists in giving his vote at election-hustings and saying: 'Behold I too have my twenty-thousandth part of a Talker in our national Palaver; will not all the gods be good to me?'—is one of the pleasantest; Nature nevertheless is kind at present; and puts it into the heads of many, almost of all. The liberty especially which has to purchase itself by social isolation, and each man standing separate from the other, having no 'business with him' but a cash account: this is such a liberty as the Earth seldom saw; as the Earth will not long put up with, recommend it how you may. This liberty turns out before long, continued in action with all men flinging up their caps round it, to be for the working Millions a liberty to die by want of food; for the Idle Thousands and Units, alas, a still more fatal liberty to live in want of work; to have no earnest duty to do in this God's World any more" — The War and unemployment have greatly added to their number to-day. "But as to universal suffrage again—can it be proved that, since the beginning of the world, there was ever given a universal vote in favour of the worthiest man or thing? John Milton, inquiring of universal England what the worth of *Paradise Lost* was, received for answer Five Pounds Sterling. George Hudson, inquiring in like manner what his services on the railways might be worth, received for answer (prompt temporary answer) Fifteen Hundred Thousand ditto. Alas, Jesus Christ asking the Jews what *he* deserved, was not the answer, Death on the Gallows!" "We may depend on it, Heaven in the most constitutional countries knows well who is a slave and who is not. And with regard to voting I lay it down as a rule: No real *slave's* vote is other than a nuisance whensoever or wheresoever or in what manner soever it be given. No *slave's* vote . . . the fact is, slaves are in a tremendous majority everywhere; and the voting of them (not to be got rid of just yet) is a nuisance in proportion, a nuisance of proportionately tremendous magnitude, properly indeed the great fountainhead of all the nuisances whatsoever." Nietzsche could not have used a more naked word to describe what the majority of men are and must be, nor denounced the potential evil of Democracy more forcibly.

On two things Carlyle seems to me to rest his doctrine of the social need of heroes, the rule of the best: "England will either learn to reverence its heroes and discriminate them from sham-heroes and valets and gas-lighted histrions, and to prize them as God's voices... or else England will continue to worship new and ever new forms of Quackland, and so, with whatever resiliences and rebounds, it matters little, go down to the Father of Quacks". The first of these is the natural desire in the heart of the great majority of men to be governed, to be guided, to obey (witness Russia and Italy and Germany to-day). Nietszche dwells always on the envy felt by the slave, the weakling, the lower classes, for the great, the strong, the wise; and there is an element of truth in this, had I time to analyse it; but a much more obvious fact is the almost pathetic readiness of the mass of men to accept leadership in things political, intellectual and spiritual. We in educational circles are always declaring that the end of education is to teach people to think for themselves. But can the majority ever do so? My experience is that eighty per cent. of a class do not want to think for themselves, nor are capable of doing so. The man who can does so from the beginning. The majority want to be taught what to think, and the practice of Communist Russia and Fascist Italy points to the same conclusion. Men can and must be taught what to think. So the Catholic Church has always taught, and so the Communist and Fascist insists to-day. Freedom of thought and of the Press have had a short and precarious history. Men desire to believe: hero-worship is not only an instinct, it is a need of the human spirit.

The other fact on which Carlyle leans is that, this being the case, and society being a complex organism, the laws of whose being are not open to every man, are only slowly being discovered even by the few, but whose laws, like all the laws of Nature, are relentless and irreversible (make no allowance for ignorance; give no place to repentance), it is folly to suppose that mechanically, through the free play of contending egoisms, or the mechanism of the ballot-box, society can be safely and wisely governed. It can only be done by giving the government to the wise, to those who have what he calls "the seeing-eye", which in political as in other practical matters anticipates the findings of science, may guide where, as Pascal taught, science will never be able to lay down fixed principles because of her abstract character. Life, social and individual, is a conflict in which Justice in the long run will prevail: in the long run, Right and Might will be found to be identi-

cal; but this brings us to the difficult question—
what did Carlyle mean by the Justice which in the
end always prevails, which he had, in the "Everlasting Yea", persuaded himself lies at the heart
of the Universe? "Effected it will be", he says,
speaking of the just regulation of labour, "unless
it were a Demon that made the Universe; which
I for my part do at no moment...in the least
believe"; and again: "All fighting, as we noticed
long ago, is the dusty conflict of strengths, each
thinking itself the strongest, or, in other words,
the justest;—of Mights which do in the long run,
and forever will in this just Universe in the long
run, mean Rights". Note the emphasis by repeti-
tion put on the "long run". Nietzsche considers
these vehement assertions to be a confession by
Carlyle that he does not really believe. "Carlyle
stupefies himself by means of the *fortissimo* of his
reverence for men of strong faith, and his rage
over those who are less foolish; he is in sore need
of noise.... At bottom he is an English Atheist
who makes it a point of honour not to be so."
And others besides Schopenhauer and Nietzsche
have doubted if justice were traceable in the
workings of the universe:

> Great is the Truth, and will prevail
> When none cares whether it prevail or not.

For in a great deal that he says about Law and the
inevitable working of things, Carlyle has in view

rather a scientific conception of Law than a moral one. He means the fact, as it is, rather than a law, of cause and effect. Things are what they are and their consequences will be what they will be. Whether one should call such an arrangement of things just or not is a question, is a judgment of Faith rather than Experience. In his talk of Law and Justice, two different strains in Carlyle's education come together, his study of science— he was an able and interested mathematician— and his earlier puritanical Old Testament upbringing. He would link the scientific law, or rather fact of cause and effect, with that other conception of Law as imposed by God, so that national prosperity is the reward, national disaster the penalty of disobedience: "And it shall come to pass, if thou shalt hearken diligently unto the voice of the Lord thy God, to observe to do all his commandments which I command thee this day, that the Lord thy God will set thee on high above all nations of the earth....Blessed shalt thou be in the city, and blessed shalt thou be in the field. Blessed shall be the fruit of thy body, and the fruit of thy ground, and the fruit of thy cattle, the increase of thy kine and the young of thy flock, etc." But there is in Carlyle's mind a link between the two conceptions, and that is this: Among these laws of the Universe, irreversible and relentless, is the social nature of man and the

29

desire ineradicable from his heart for justice in his social relations. That too is a cause which has to be reckoned with. Man is bound to his fellows by more than a cash nexus. Carlyle in *Past and Present* returns again and again to the instance of the Irish widow who, refused charity on every hand, proved her common humanity by infecting the lane with typhus fever, whereof seventeen people died. In treating men as isolated atoms, connected only by the mutual attraction and repulsion of money-making, society is ignoring the real nature of man and sinning against the law of justice. Here the two conceptions become one. Justice is the demand of every human heart: "It is not what a man outwardly has or wants that constitutes the happiness or misery of him. Nakedness, Hunger, Distress of all kinds, Death itself, he has cheerfully suffered when the heart was right. It is the feeling of injustice that is insupportable to all men. The brutalest black African cannot bear that he should be treated unjustly. No man can bear it or ought to bear it". The French Revolution was to Carlyle an event that justified the ways of God to men because it was a long delayed, but finally achieved vindication of the poor and the unjustly treated, as it had seemed to the young Wordsworth. But the doctrine of justice has another implication for Carlyle that is not so commonly found; here

30

Carlyle draws nearer to Nietzsche. The desire for justice is the vindication not only of the poor man when he rises at last in rebellion. It also, Carlyle seems to think, is the vindication of the strong man, the Hero, even of the conqueror, for "no man at bottom means injustice. It is always for some obscure distorted image of a right that he contends...could a man own to himself that the thing he fought for was wrong, contrary to fairness and the law of reason, he would also own that it thereby stood condemned and hopeless: he could fight for it no longer". Your great conquerors are not inspired purely by greed of possession and lust of power.* They were not merely destructive forces like Attila. However they may have erred, what moved them was an instinct of right, a belief that they could order things better, make a better use of what they conquered, and they are to be judged by the result. So Carlyle seems to think, though as we shall see, he is a little uneasy about some of his heroes. Dr Johnson said that he *loved* the University of Salamanca because, when asked by the Pope if it were just to conquer America, that University alone replied, NO. Carlyle would not have agreed, and it

* That is the difference between the true Conqueror and the bucanier: "Victory is the aim of each. But deep in the heart of the noble man it lies forever legible that as an Invisible Just God made him, so will and must God's Justice and this only, were it never so invisible, ultimately prosper in all controversies and enterprises whatsoever". *Past and Present*, III. 10; and see III. 13.

31

is clearly a very difficult question to answer in the abstract whether it had been juster to leave America to contending tribes of Red Indians, or the South Sea Islands to such amiable cannibals as Melville describes in *Omoo*, or to clear them out and to establish such a civilisation as that of America to-day with all its complexities of good and evil.

But it is just this complex nature of human society, the difficulty of deciding what is just and then getting it done, that makes the need of a Hero so insistent; and what I wish to consider is Carlyle's conception of the Hero, especially in the field of action, on whom it is that his choice falls, and the significance of that choice. When we turn to *On Heroes, Hero-Worship and the Heroic in History*, we find, of course, that there are different types of the Hero, Heroes in different spheres of human activity. All the leaders of men have not been Kings or Captains. Some have been Prophets and Poets. The various classes that Carlyle distinguished for the purpose of his lectures will be found, I think, to fall into the two main classes of King and Prophet. Carlyle has little interest in poets who are not also prophets. He cannot away with a Keats who seems to him to be the artist alone, and therefore a Hedonist.* A German

* "Milnes has written", he comments in 1848, "this year a book on Keats. This remark to make on it: 'An attempt to

32

writer on *Helden und Dichter* has made, I think,
a clearer distinction of three main classes—the
men of action, the Kings as Carlyle would say,
Alexander, Caesar, Napoleon: the heroes of the
spiritual life, prophets who have created a tradition of Being, Suffering and Teaching, Buddha,
Christ and Mahomet; and lastly the Heroes
who live in their work, their creation, their word
—as Dante, Shakespeare, Goethe, and one might
add surely heroes such as Rembrandt, Beethoven.
But the hero that Carlyle as a social reformer
was chiefly concerned with was the Hero as King,

make us eat dead dog by exquisite currying and cooking.
Wont eat it. A truly unwise little book. The kind of man that
Keats was gets ever more horrible to me. Force of hunger for
pleasure of every kind, and want of all other force—that is a
combination! Such a structure of soul, it would once have been
very evident, was a chosen 'Vessel of Hell', and truly for ever
there is justice in that feeling. At present we try to love and
pity, and even worship, such a soul there being enough of
similarity. Away with it! There is perhaps no clearer evidence
of our universal immorality and cowardly untruth than even in
such sympathies." A sweeping and a cruel judgment, and
quaint, if one thinks, coming from the unlimited admirer of
Burns whose love of pleasure was as keen as Keats's and his
recklessness in its pursuit far greater. "We have said",
writes Scott, who had known more of Burns's life than Carlyle, "that Robert Burns was the child of impulse and feeling.
Of the steady principle which cleaves to that which is good, he
was unfortunately divested by the violence of those passions
which finally wrecked him. It is most affecting to add, that
while swimming, struggling, and finally yielding to the torrent,
he never lost sight of the beacon which ought to have guided
him, yet never profited by its light." Whether either the one
or the other be right there can be no doubt that Scott's is the
more charitable judgment. Charity, Carlyle had come to think,
was a weakness.

and it is he that presents the chief difficulties in the study of the Hero. To the others I must make only a passing reference.

Now Carlyle's choice of a Hero in this field is very illuminating. He touches on Mirabeau and Napoleon, and he was to write the Life of Frederick, but there is only one Hero whom he accepts with his whole heart, and that is Oliver Cromwell.

But before speaking of Cromwell, let me just say a word on one of Carlyle's heroes because he illustrates what one might call the lowest common denominator of the hero, and that is Dr Johnson, a rather strange figure in this setting, if Burns is a stranger. Carlyle places Johnson among the Men of Letters, but it is *not* as a great writer, or as the "Great Moralist" of the *Rambler* whom Boswell revered, that he gives him his place, but "in virtue of his sincerity, his speaking still in some sort from the heart of Nature, . . . that Johnson was a prophet". But sincerity hardly describes exactly what Carlyle means. Pepys was, I think, sincere. What he means by Johnson speaking from the heart of Nature is that Johnson spoke and thought from the depths of his own nature, was absolutely in-different to what others around him thought or said. With all his prejudices, Johnson is a Hero in that his own soul was his guide through life. For the fashions of the day in thought or history he cared not a whit. Others might be sceptics, or Whigs, because that was the right thing for an "enlightened" man to be: Johnson was a believer and a Tory. "Clear your mind of cant", was his watchword, and so in his small way he was a centre of force, a fountainhead; and this is the first, the basal note of the Hero. He is neither impelled nor inhibited by others. His thoughts, his deeds, his words are his own. The great Disciple, as we might describe another class of men, may achieve much— sometimes even effect what the master failed in— St Paul, Abu Bekr, Augustus. But each has caught his inspiration from a master, looks back to him, acknowledges him as master even after his death.

Oliver Cromwell is the one historical man of action for whom Carlyle has no apology to make in the *Lectures*; and to clearing of Cromwell's character, and establishing his fame, he devoted years of research; producing, Professor Trevelyan declares, in *Oliver Cromwell's Letters and Speeches* his most original and solid contribution to history.[*] It is a strange work. Cromwell is never censured, never made responsible for the ultimate failure of the Commonwealth. Carlyle accompanies his speeches with a running comment of approving interjection in a manner that used to be customary

[*] But see the edition of this work by S. C. Lomas, 1904 and *Carlyle, His Rise and Fall*, by Norwood Young, 1927.

in Methodist churches. The failure of Cromwell to make good in the end, the "blessed Restoration" which brought back Charles II and the era of Nell Gwynns, etc., is for Carlyle the great tragedy in English history. "Oliver is gone; and with him English Puritanism, laboriously built together by this man, and made a thing far-shining to its own Century and memorable to all Centuries, soon goes. Puritanism without its King is *kingless*, anarchic; King, Defender of the Puritan Faith, there can now none be found;— and nothing is left but to recall the old disowned Defender with the remnants of his Four Surplices and Two Centuries of *Hypocrisis* (or Play-acting *not* so called), and put up with that, the best we may. The Genius of England no longer soars Sunward, world-defiant, like an Eagle through the storms, mewing her mighty youth, as John Milton saw her do: the Genius of England much liker a greedy Ostrich intent on provender and a whole skin mainly, stands with its *other* extremity sunward; with its Ostrich-head stuck into the readiest bush, of old Church-tippets, Kings-cloaks, or whatever other sheltering Fallacy there may be, and *so* awaits the issue. The issue has been slow; but it now seems to have been inevitable. No Ostrich, intent on gross terrene provender and sticking its head into Fallacies, but will be awakened one day—in a terrible *a posteriori* manner if not otherwise! Awake before it comes to that; gods and men bid us awake! The Voices of our Fathers, with thousandfold stern monition to one and all, bid us awake."

Carlyle's choice of Cromwell as Hero is luminous, because in him the two strains of thought in his conception of Justice, Law, combine. Cromwell had "the seeing eye" that gained the victory for the Puritan Rebellion, because he saw what things are and what their consequences will be, while others were lost in the tangles of constitutional or ecclesiastical theory: "I beseech you in the bowels of Christ, think it possible you may be mistaken", as Cromwell said to the Scottish Presbyterians of Scotland, in their eyes alone orthodox, alone righteous. He drove through where others discussed abstract rights. But he was also the first of Heroes, because he was the soldier of God, had, as no other of the great soldiers of history, a moral and religious end: "To see God's own law, then universally acknowledged for complete as it stood in the Holy Written Book, made good in this World; to see this, or the true unwearied aim and struggle towards this: it was a thing worth living for and dying for! Eternal Justice: that God's will be done on Earth as it is in Heaven: corollaries enough will flow from that, if that be there; if that be not there, no corollary good for much will flow. It was the general spirit of England in the Seventeenth Century". But alas! it is difficult not to feel that Carlyle is deceiving himself about this union of qualities in Cromwell. The man who believes as Cromwell did that he finds the whole law of God written in any book, that in all he did, the dispersion of the Parliament which had given him his power, the execution of the King, he is following the leading of God; who finds God's sanction for all his doings, for the victories he has gained from Marston Moor, Naseby, Drogheda, Tredah, Dunbar, to the "crowning mercy" of Worcester, that man has lost the "seeing eye", and is walking in a vain illusion which will bring its consequences. One may or may not defend all these actions on prudential grounds or grounds of necessity, but to claim divine inspiration for every deed of violence is a dangerous thing. When he has finished describing how all the Friars were knocked on the head at Tredah, Cromwell goes on: "And now give me leave to say how it comes to pass that this work was wrought. It was set upon some of our hearts that a great thing should be done, not by power or might, but by the spirit of God. And is it not so clearly?" Comment which gives Carlyle much solemn satisfaction: "An armed soldier solemnly conscious to himself that he is a Soldier of God the Just—a consciousness which it well beseems all soldiers and all men to have;—armed soldier terrible as death, relentless as doom; doing God's judgments on the enemies of God...art thou worthy to love such a thing; worthy to do other than hate it or shriek over it?" One is tempted to ask Carlyle: "Are you yourself really justifying the action, or are you taking refuge from a decision in a cloud of words that would have one meaning for your mother and another for yourself?" Does Carlyle really believe with the Jews that God's will is written down in black and white to the last tittle, known to us definitely, that obedience to this known law is the guarantee of prosperity, all misfortune a punishment for the neglect of this known law? The result of that for the Jews was that when One came who believed he had a deeper insight into the Will of God, they felt bound by the Law of God to account him a blasphemer and crucify one who claimed to be the Son of God. Even in Cromwell's age there were those who did not think that God's Will was thus known and written down, but believed that God had given us reason wherewith to explore it— that was the tenor of Hooker's *Ecclesiastical Polity*. It is, I fear, what Carlyle most admired in Cromwell that most distinctly marks his limitation as a Hero, his fanaticism—or if his personal fanaticism was less than his language suggests, his too great dependance on the fanatical element

39

in his following, so that he could not free himself
and the country from the tyranny of Saints and
Major Generals. The sword of the spirit and of
steel had placed him where he was and could alone
uphold him:

> And for the last effect
> Still keep the sword erect:
> Besides the force it has to fright
> The spirits of the shady night,
> The same arts that did gain
> A pow'r must it maintain.

Yet it is a prejudiced, short-sighted person who
would deny heroic stature to Cromwell. He is in
a sense the one Hero in our history, this man who
when already middle-aged, untrained in arms or
diplomacy, rose by the innate force of character
and genius to be the ruler of the English people,
the conqueror of Ireland and Scotland, and who
made the name of England feared and respected
throughout Europe. In some ways he did more
than Napoleon, for no revolution had reduced
England to the condition from which Napoleon
rescued France, and he made himself master of
a people with an ingrained constitutionalism of
mind, a passion for at least the appearance of in-
herited right, so that even Cromwell's Parlia-
ments would not get to business, but must waste
time and weary out his patience debating *their*
right and *his* right. His power had to rely on the
sword, and when he died the order of things he

had established melted away, and even by the Whigs, Cromwell was remembered as the "great, bad man" Clarendon had called him, though a bad man who communicated his own power to the people he ruled. "These disturbers", says Burke, "were not so much like men usurping power as asserting their natural place in society. Their rising was to illuminate and beautify the world. Their conquest over their competitors was by outshining them. The hand that like a destroying angel smote the country communicated to it the force and energy under which it suffered. I do not say (God forbid), I do not say that the virtues of such men are to be taken as a balance to their crimes; but they were some corrective to their effects...such was, as I said, our Cromwell." It was left for Carlyle to do for Cromwell what Mommsen has done for Caesar.*

But Carlyle's choice of Cromwell is an interesting and instructive one in several ways. If, as I think, this cult of the Hero, especially on its religious side, was in part a result of Carlyle's early enthusiasm for Novalis and the German Romantics yet his insistence on the moral requirement is characteristic not only of Carlyle but of the British people, especially the English, generally. They have at no time been altogether willing to

* Mommsen's conclusions are not accepted by all historians. See Prof. Conway's article in the *Quarterly Review*, July, 1933.

accept the strong man as the arbiter of their destinies—even Cromwell found the English a stiff-necked generation—and they have always required their leaders to present their moral testimonials. Even in the sphere of the Prophet, a Knox and a Calvin were more wholeheartedly accepted as Prophets in Switzerland, France and Scotland than in England. The Anglican Church through Hooker appealed to reason and tradition; the Independent or Quaker vindicated in different ways and measures the claim of the individual's experience, the "inner light". The acceptance of Napoleon in France was at first practical, the need of peace and order, but the practical demand was soon intensified by the French love of "La Gloire", which in the twelfth and thirteenth centuries had given Europe the cult of chivalry. But Germany is the home of the mystical worship of the Hero. It is hard to believe that a German could endorse Bernard Shaw's recent dictum on Napoleon that it would be better if he had never lived. It would seem to him almost blasphemous. A man like Napoleon, they would say, is not to be measured by a moral yard-stick; and if the blood he shed condemns him might not the Hero as Prophet be in danger of condemnation—Mahomet, even Christ: "I came not to send peace on earth; I came not to send peace but a sword". These are not the least true words that he uttered. To Nietzsche, Napoleon represents the passion of new spiritual possibilities, and he cites Taine on Napoleon as the reincarnation of the great man of the Renaissance: "Suddenly the master faculty reveals itself; the artist which was latent in the politician comes forth from his scabbard; he creates *dans l'idéal et l'impossible*. He is once more recognised as that which he is: the posthumous brother of Dante and of Michael Angelo; and verily in view of the definite contours of his vision, the intensity, the coherence and inner consistency of his dream, the depth of his meditations, the super-human greatness of his conception, he is their equal... *il est un des trois esprits souverains de la renaissance*". To Carlyle Napoleon is but half a hero; to Lord Morley he was only a Corsican brigand of transcendent ability and transcendent good fortune.

But instead of Napoleon, I will for the moment take another Hero of the continent in whom also one can study the contradictions in the estimation of the Hero, and that is Julius Caesar. The most vivid exponent of German Hero-worship to-day, the late Professor Gundolf, has written a history of the fame of Caesar from his own day to the end of the nineteenth century, and it is very instructive. The greatness of Caesar as soldier and statesman and man was felt and acknowledged from his own day even by his enemies, and not only his greatness, but the charm of his personality—his magnanimity, what one might call his *style* in life and writings. Napoleon, at close quarters, exercised no such fascination over men like Talleyrand, Fouché and others as Caesar did over Cicero and Brutus. Caesar was a *gentleman*, which Napoleon with all his greatness was not. And Caesar's star has never set. In all ages have been men willing to echo Antony's words in Shakespeare's play:

> Thou art the ruins of the noblest man
> That ever lived in the tide of time.

In the Middle Ages, Caesar became more of a formula than a personality, the founder of the Empire; but with the Renaissance his personality revived. The greatness of Caesar, says Gundolf, was rediscovered by Petrarch; his charm by Montaigne. "When I reflect", says the latter, "upon his incomparable greatness of soul, I can excuse victory for not having been able to shake off his fetters even in that very unjust and iniquitous cause."*

But Montaigne's closing words bring us face to face with the other side of Caesar's reputation

---

* "On parle beaucoup de la fortune de Caesar; mais cet homme extraordinaire avait tant de grands qualités sans pas un défaut, quoiqu'il eut bien des vices, qu'il eût été bien difficile que, quelque armée qu'il eût commande, il n'eût été vainqueur et que en quelque république qu'il fût né il ne l'eût gouvernée." Montaigne.

throughout the centuries, leaving the Middle Ages out of the count. As Cromwell by Clarendon, Caesar, by the moralists of his own and succeeding ages, moralists and constitutionalists, was accounted a *great but a bad man*. This two-fold judgment goes back to Cicero. "Cicero's picture of Caesar", says Gundolf, "varies like the colours of an opal from that of a god to that of a knave. In eulogistic speeches he treats him as the glory of his age, speeches in which he celebrates his exploits in war, his magnanimity, his power of intellect, in a more sincerely elevated strain than any writer has done since; and that not only to Caesar's face, when he is speaking as the flattering pleader for his clients and himself . . . or under the influence of a concealed anxiety before this enigmatically mild man whose power he knew, but even after his death, in an outbreak of feeling, oppressed by hatred, sated with revenge, moved even against his will with admiration. In the *Second Philippic*, it is true, Caesar's mighty shadow is evoked to put to shame Antony strutting in the mantle of the giant; yet the conjuration is no mere rhetorical trick, but expresses Cicero's conviction. Thus has he seen Caesar through all the oscillations of party feeling and personal relations—a miracle of power, of intellect, of refinement, of completeness—and withal the reckless destroyer of the state and corrupter of the people." That is the judgment which passed down the centuries till the nineteenth; and over against the Great Man appeared the Moral Man, the virtuous Hero, Cato or Brutus:

> *Victrix causa deis placuit, sed victa Catoni;*
>   Where is now the soul
> Of God-like Cato? He that durst be good
> When Caesar durst be evil; and had power
> As not to live his slave, to die his master?
> Or where the constant Brutus, that being proof
> Against all charm of benefits did strike
> So brave a blow into the monster's heart
> That sought unkindly to captive his Country?
> O they are fled the light!...
>   ...nothing good
> Gallant or great: tis true that Cordus says
> "Brave Cassius was the last of all that race."

So speaks the old Roman republican in Ben Jonson's *Sejanus,* and you have there the idealisation of the virtuous hero, the Harry Vanes and Lafayettes with whom Carlyle can at times grow impatient, even if it is with some uneasiness that he accepts as hero one who is not also good, and prefers Cromwell to Caesar or Napoleon because of his more religious and moral aim. It is a rather puzzling dilemma this presented by the great man who does great things and the good man often apparently quite inefficient but nevertheless "good".

46

The gordian knot, if it is one, is cut of course by Nietzsche, who denies validity to the "good" as thus conceived. If Ruskin led to Oscar Wilde, as a recent French critic declares, Carlyle led direct to Nietzsche. His superman is a further development of the Hero. Might is right, says Carlyle, because in the long run, if it is not also right, the might will prove delusive. He blends, as I have said, a scientific with a religious pronouncement. If the power you rely on is not a power in nature you must fail; if you have made a mistake your air-ship will fall; or, to speak religiously, if you are violating the fundamental instinct of justice, if you are not acting in accordance with God's Will, you must be defeated. Nietzsche, accepting from his first teacher Schopenhauer the doctrine that there is *no* providential order in the world, no law revealed and sanctioned by a power external to man, obedience to which is rewarded, disobedience punished, as set forth so clearly in the Book of Deuteronomy, that we are our own guides and create our own values, Nietzsche takes the step and declares Might is Right. Ultimately it is the only Right, imposed on the mass, *das Gesindel*, by the superior class and accepted by them. If morality becomes something different, then it is a kind of miasma rising *from* the mass and paralysing the strong, the authentically good, a device by which the Will to Power that is in us

47

all, directed by the priest, the strong in craft though wanting in nobility and courage, succeeds in restraining the strong and noble, dragging all down to the anarchic level of equality, or, under the disguise of doing so, subjecting the generous and noble warrior to the crafty and revengeful priest, so that the Emperor comes to Canossa. Christianity especially has been one long conspiracy of the weak against the strong, exalting the so-called virtues of humility, meekness, pity, over the natural and essential virtues of strength, pride, and courage. Nietzsche indeed pushes the superiority of the great man to all morality so far that one feels tempted to find his supermen to-day in gentlemen like Mr Hatry and others, (who, having risen beyond good and evil, are now serving their time,) or at least in the oil or rubber or newspaper magnates of modern trade. Nor indeed would he quite deny the affinity of the hero to the criminal. "Dostoievsky," he writes, "this profound man...found the Siberian convicts among whom he lived for many years...those thoroughly hopeless criminals for whom no road back to society stood open—very different from what even he had expected—that is to say, carved from the best, hardest, and most valuable material that grows on Russian soil." "The criminal type", he says again, "is the type of the strong man amid unfavourable conditions, a strong man made sick.... Almost every genius knows the Catilinarian Life as one of the stages in his development, a feeling of hate, revenge, revolt against everything that exists, that has ceased to evolve—Catiline—the early stage of every Caesar". But Nietzsche would not, I think, have admitted to the rank of Hero merely the great capitalist, the profiteer, for he sees one of the perils to society in their lack of distinction, of any claim to superiority beyond their great wealth. They cannot evoke the sentiment of hero-worship.

But it is not my intention to follow Nietzsche in the quest of the superman, compared with whom all the heroes of history gradually lost interest, so that he could not disguise his contempt for Carlyle's devout attitude: "Never yet has there been a superman. Naked I considered the greatest and least of men—all too like were they the one to the other; truly even the greatest I found—*all too human*".

I think that the difference, if there is one, between the English and the Continental attitude towards the Hero is explicable without going quite so far. It is partly a symptom of the Continental inclination to allow a more absolute value to what appeals to the imagination than *we* are altogether willing to do. In judging of both men and works of art, we are more unwilling to allow an absolute value to anything that does not justify itself on practical or on moral grounds. By the German, the French and the Italian critic, the greatness, the sheer abstract greatness, of a man like Caesar or Napoleon, his force of intellect and will, is accorded an admiration, that we are more disposed to modify by a demand that he shall approve himself also by his moral worth, just as in art they are more ready to admire and accept a great work without submitting it to the test of moral value, at least as measurable by fixed and recognised standards. Things and men that appeal to the imagination have thereby worth. To deny the greatness of Caesar or Napoleon is as blasphemous or foolish as to deny the greatness of the sea or the tempest:

> What! alive and so bold, O Earth?
>   Art thou not overbold?
> What! leapest thou forth as of old
> In the light of thy morning mirth,
> The last of the flock of the starry fold?
> Ha! leapest thou forth as of old?
> Are not the limbs still when the ghost is fled,
> And canst thou move Napoleon being dead?

Shelley catches there, as a poet might, whatever his final judgment on Napoleon, the sense of his greatness not to be ignored. To Mr Shaw and Mr Wells as much as to Carlyle such a feeling is repellent. The moral judgment is insistent. Carlyle can with difficulty overlook the youthful immoralities of his hero Frederick: they would not have weighed with Goethe for a minute. Even Sir Walter Scott, whose imagination so much dominated his view of history, is yet well aware that the final estimate must be moral and practical. His Claverhouse makes but a poor defence of his conduct to Morton. Scott refused to write the Life of Mary Queen of Scots, so well aware was he that his judgment and imagination were not on the same side. He is far more of a Jacobite in his letters to Miss Clephane than in the novels that close with *Redgauntlet* in such a clear perception of the fatal flaw of character which was the doom of a House, the best of whom had, as Laud admitted, neither greatness nor the capacity to be made great.

But this is not all. There is another explanation of this difficulty of reconciling greatness and goodness in the Hero. The antinomy of Great but Bad man may be due to a too abstract conception of both "greatness" and "goodness", the Hero and the Moral Man. The moral man, Cato and Brutus and Harry Vane and Lafayette is, as Carlyle too feels, a rather empty ideal. Cato is approved, Caesar condemned, by the application of a very abstract standard of Platonic and Stoic Virtue. I do not know why it is that the word "virtue", "virtuous", so much in favour in the eighteenth century, has so much lost colour, if it be not due to this distrust of abstract virtues and moral commandments whether engraved on stone or painted in our chancels, with the appropriate penalties expressed or implied. "Thou shalt not kill"—"Penalty, a drop not exceeding twelve feet"! Or the sanction may be more purely prudential:

> Do not adultery commit;
> Advantage rarely comes of it.

And it has been the mission of the Hero as Prophet to wage war against such legalism and substitute for it the less definite but more searching rule: "Thou shalt love the Lord thy God with all thy heart, etc., and thy neighbour as thyself". But the Hero also has often been considered too much in the abstract of an aesthetic admiration of his gifts and exploits. Plutarch was mainly taken up with such descriptions of his qualities, interlarded with all the indications of his favour in the eyes of the Gods, the oracles and other signs and wonders that accompanied his career or his death. It was only gradually that the question became not what were his personal qualities, intellectual or moral, but what did he achieve of permanent worth for his nation or for civilisation generally. Gundolf traces the rise of this demand to the constitutional wars of England, but the English approach to the question was, he thinks, too strictly practical and legal. It was Montesquieu who first, taking the ruler in close relation to his people, brought this aspect of the Hero to the front; and one result of it, in the survey of the heroes of antiquity, was, Gundolf points out, that for a time Alexander was given a place superior to Caesar because he had rendered real service to humanity as the bulwark of the West against the East and the disseminator of Hellenic civilisation, whereas Caesar was still held to be the destroyer of the liberty of Gaul and of his own country. It remained for Mommsen and the historians of the nineteenth century to vindicate Caesar both as the conqueror of Gaul, and as the founder of the Empire, to show that it was Caesar and not the virtuous constitutionalists who had the "seeing eye" which Carlyle exalts as the special gift of the Hero. It was but natural that Froude, the disciple of Carlyle, followed Mommsen in the glorification of Caesar, and looking round for another hero, was tempted to try his hand at Henry VIII.

Now this estimate of the Hero had established itself before Carlyle wrote, and underlies all he has to say on the subject, as it does, say, Mr Wells' reconsideration of various heroes. If we now mean anything by a Hero it is, I suppose, someone who has quite definitely, we believe, carried mankind a step forward, hard as it may be to decide what are the real steps in advance that humanity has taken. But what I wish to suggest now is that, from this point of view, one may perceive the reason of the difference between the British and the Continental conception of the Hero, and understand why Carlyle and the English writers generally have laid greater stress on the moral aspects of his character and work, than for example Machiavelli in *The Prince*, or the Continent generally in their estimate of Napoleon. The Hero as King, as ruler and soldier, is to some extent the creation of an emergency, the saviour. The emergency will not always produce him, witness the Italy of Dante and Machiavelli, but the emergency is the great man's opportunity. In peril of its existence a nation is more willing to place its fate in his hands, as the Dutch in 1672, the French after the Revolution, and say Germany when Bismarck came to the top or at the present juncture. Dante had looked for a saviour from beyond the Alps; Machiavelli had hoped to find him in Cesare Borgia. We have been hitherto less often in such a predicament, perhaps, as our Continental critics say, because of our insular position; and we have been able to "muddle through" our constitutional crises without his aid; for in the ordinary course of political business, a cabinet of Heroes is as little to be looked for as a cabinet of Archangels, and might prove as ineffectual as a Cabinet of all the Talents. And this may explain also the almost mystical reverence of Continental writers for Napoleon whom, with a few striking exceptions, English critics have never quite accepted as a Hero, a Benefactor. The Continental admiration is not purely imaginative and artistic. To western Europe Napoleon, if in the end he became the enemy and so the quickener of national feeling, was at the outset both a deliverer and a promise—a deliverer from what Shelley calls the old Anarch Custom and the promise of a United Europe, one who might do for Europe what Machiavelli had hoped Borgia would do for Italy. Byron, who understood the European point of view as few Englishmen at the time did, has put that thought into four lines:

A single step into the right had made
This man the Washington of worlds betrayed;
A single step into the wrong has given
His name a doubt to all the winds of heaven.

That is the feeling which inspires Nietzsche's admiration of Napoleon, "that synthesis of Monster and Superman". "What I am concerned with —for I see it preparing itself slowly and hesitatingly—is the United Europe. It was the only real work, the one impulse in the soul of all the broadminded and deep-thinking men of this century—the preparation of a new synthesis, the tentative effort to anticipate the future of the European. Only in their weaker moments, when they grew old, did they fall back again into the national narrowness of the Fatherlander—then they were once more *patriots*—I am thinking of men like Napoleon, Heine, Goethe, Stendhal, Schopenhauer.... Enough; here as in other matters the coming century will be found following in the footsteps of Napoleon—the first man and the man of greatest initiative and advanced views of modern times."

If the Hero be in part the child of the emergency, to ask that he should always also be a good man is to say that in a political emergency we can always act in accordance with principles that are sufficient for normal conditions. It is more; it is to assume that we know more completely what is right, what is good than perhaps is the truth. Even the Hero as Prophet has presented himself as a challenge to the standards of his day; has not been at once accepted as a Saint, but as a blasphemer and a friend of Publicans and Sinners. And he too is the response, to some extent, to the emergency—Mahomet, Christ. One aspect of the social and moral conditions of man when Christ appeared is supplied by St Paul in the *Epistle to the Romans*, supported by the evidence of the satirists. "The pictures so constructed are mosaics of singular vices, and they have led to the not unnatural impression that those centuries constituted an era of exceptional wickedness." But the late Edwin Hatch in the Hibbert Lectures for 1888 showed that there was another aspect of the emergency: "that the age in which Christianity grew was in reality an age of moral reformation. There was the growth of a higher religious morality, which believed that God was pleased by moral action rather than by sacrifice. There was the growth of a belief that life requires amendment". It was the age of Epictetus. And if the great men who were captains and kings are to be judged solely by the blood they shed, what of the Prophets? In their name rivers of blood have been poured out.

The late Lord Acton thought that most great men in the field of politics and warfare had been more or less bad men; Swift thought that they had been *lunatics*: "For, if we take a survey of the greatest actions that have been performed in the world, under the influence of single men; which are the establishment of new empires by conquest; the advance and progress of new schemes in philosophy; and the contriving as well as the propagating of new religions—we shall find the authors of them all to have been persons whose natural reason hath admitted great revolutions from their diet, their education, the prevalency of some certain temper, together with the particular influence of air and climate. . . . For the brain in its natural position and state of serenity disposeth its owner to pass his life in the *common* forms, without any thought of subduing multitudes to his power, his reasons or his visions; and the more he shapes his understanding by the pattern of human learning the less he is inclined to form parties after his particular notions, because that instructs him in his private infirmities as well as in the stubborn ignorance of the people". Carlyle but a few years ago was reckoned a mightily discredited prophet. The editor of the Centenary Edition of his works, the late H. D. Traill, could affirm in the opening introduction with confidence that: "Carlyle is neither prophet nor ethical doctor, but simply a great master of literature who lives for posterity by the art which he despised". When a few years later he came to introduce *Past and Present*, he could boast complacently that: "this pronouncement. . .has on the whole been received with a greater amount of assent, express or tacit, than one would have ventured to count on when the sentence was penned", and for final confirmation he appeals to the very work in hand, *Past and Present*.* Such was

* "It is with some unwillingness that we pass from this picturesque and romantic episode to the two concluding books, and find ourselves at hand-grips with professors of the dismal science, commercial capitalists, *laissez-faire* theorists, Plugson

58

our complacent mood before the War. Will anyone say to-day, when we are standing amid the wreck of that industrial order which Carlyle arraigned, and of that democracy at which he scoffed, that he was no prophet? "Let inventive men cease to spend their existence incessantly contriving how cotton can be made cheaper; and try to invent, a little, how cotton at its present cheapness could be more justly divided among us." Is not that the problem with which we are faced to-day, grown infinitely more pressing? And what of democracy in the Europe of Lenin and Stalin and Mussolini and Hitler and smaller varieties of the Hero type? Or the United States and Roosevelt? The feelings with which Russian and Italian and German turn appealingly to the Hero show the same blend of religious mysticism and economic demand as Carlyle felt and pro-

of Undershot, Sir Jabesh Windbag, and the rest of Carlyle's favourite bogles. They are all fallen silent—all gone dead to-day, etc." It is strange to see how many of them have come alive again—professors of the dismal science were never so much in evidence, if a little less confident than of old; commercial capitalists leading us the same glorious round from fortunes made to fortunes lost in the twinkling of an eye; and all the problems not solved and done with as Mr Traill was confident but very much alive. A Government of Business Men—there is not much cry for that to-day! They had been so shortsighted in their own sphere, made such a melancholy mess of their own and other people's money that in America they were in the recent Presidential election discredited, and for once in history Plato's philosophers, or at least University professors, are being allowed an innings—how long it will last remains to be seen.

claimed. Men will worship the great man but they will demand of him (as of their God) that he feed them. He must find them loaves and fishes. And in our own country from different angles Sir Oswald Mosley and Sir Stafford Cripps point the same road. So far as democracy and constitutional government and liberty are concerned there is not a pin to choose between them.

What Carlyle would have thought of the happenings in Russia, Italy and Germany to-day is hard to say, for he was never quite unaffected by his humours and prejudices. He would certainly not have joined in the varied and inconsistent outcries of horror, for since the War we have been divided, in the most odd manner, into those who approve of certain things done in Russia and regard them with horror when they are transferred to Italy or Germany, and *vice versa* those who accept them with complacency when directed against Socialists in Italy or Germany but shrink with horror from the same cruelties in wicked Russia. One can hardly doubt that Carlyle would have seen in the War and all that has followed it the fruits of *laissez-faire* and Democracy. Competition for trade, the cash nexus as the sole link, had failed between nations as between individuals in the state. And Democracy? A Society to promote what was called Democratic Control was instituted as the war drew on and people were growing weary. I remember putting myself sadly through a catechism. Why could neither France nor Italy afford (perhaps Britain *might* have done so) to make a reasonable peace with concessions on all sides, say in 1917? Democratic Control. No government could have gone to the people and said "the War has brought us no gain, only the *status quo ante*". Why was the Peace of Versailles so much worse than the Peace of Paris of 1814–15? Democratic Control. Recall the election and the promises extracted from candidates to exact reparations and hang the Kaiser. Why did America fail to implement President Wilson's signature and insist on leaving Europe to stew in its own juice? Democratic Control. It is part of the cant of the moment, when we have all grown wise after the event, that Lord Grey declared War without consulting the people. If it had been possible to do so they would have voted for War. The fear was not that we should be brought in but that we should leave France in the lurch, especially among the generous young whose successors are now so critical of their elders. What Carlyle would have thought of the particular Heroes themselves is even more difficult to say. He was not quick to discover heroic traits in a contemporary. And the Hero, to-day as ever, presents the same dual aspect, good and evil. If in measuring that good and evil we may be misled, as I have suggested, by too abstract standards alike of goodness and greatness, the problem yet remains. But the solution is after all perhaps not so difficult. The good and evil in what your hero does—Caesar, Augustus, William of Orange, Cromwell, Napoleon, Frederick—remains and each bears its fruit. Good may outweigh the evil. It cannot annul it. No hero in the world of action but has left behind a legacy of evil as well as good. There is only one class of Heroes who can plead that if they have achieved no great exploits, they have done no harm; they have come to us only in the attractive power of love and beauty, and that is the Hero as Poet—Dante, Shakespeare, Goethe. There is no debit side to their credit balance as there is to so many, not only Caesar and Napoleon, but, may one say it, St Paul and Mahomet. Even of the Prophet the most enduring of the victories he achieves may prove to be not those which were won for him by arms or inquisitions, but by the penetrating and pervasive influence of his character and words, the poet in the prophet. But the Hero as Poet made small appeal to Carlyle unless he could also class him as Prophet. It is strange indeed that Carlyle did not rather concentrate on the Hero as Prophet; but that he did not, but was more intent on the Hero as King, bespeaks his own sense of the emergency of his time; like Plato he would fain have ruled men, at least guided them, for that seemed to him the want of his age; and ours is confirming his forecast. We are paying dear to-day for *laissez-faire*, for refusing, while we had the wealth, the natural demand, as he affirms it in *Past and Present*, of every working man for two things, a living wage and security of employment. Even our Insurance for Unemployment came too late, and had not accumulated the funds needed for the emergency which has overtaken us. It is Carlyle who has led me, rather contrary to my own expectation, away from the Hero as Poet, which would have been my more natural theme; but he who sets out to write a lecture knows little of where and how it will end.

CAMBRIDGE: PRINTED BY
W. LEWIS, M.A.
AT THE UNIVERSITY PRESS